THE SCIENCE OF THE AURA

An Introduction to the Study of the Human Aura

THE SCIENCE OF THE AURA

An Introduction to the Study of the Human Aura

S.G.J. Ouseley

PILGRIMS PUBLISHING
Varanasi•Kathmandu

THE SCIENCE OF THE AURA

By S.G.J. Ouseley

Published by
PILGRIMS PUBLISHING

An imprint of
PILGRIMS BOOK HOUSE
B 27/98 A-8, Nawabganj Road
Durga Kund
Varanasi, India 221010
Tel: 91-542-314060, 312496
Fax: 91-542-314059
E-mail: pilgrims@satyam.net.in

Distributed in India by
BOOK FAITH INDIA
414-416 Express Tower
Azadpur Commercial Complex
New Delhi-110033, India
Tel: 91-11-713-2459
Fax: 91-11-724-9674
E-mail: pilgrim@del2.vsnl.net.in

Distributed in Nepal by
PILGRIMS BOOK HOUSE
P.O Box 3872
Kathmandu, Nepal
Tel: 977-1-424942
Fax: 977-1-424943
E-mail: pilgrims@wlink.com.np

First published in London in 1949 by
L.N. Flower & Co Ltd.

Copyright © 2000 Pilgrims Publishing
All Rights Reserved

ISBN 81-7769-021-3

Edited by C.N. Burchett
Layout by Hom KC
Cover design by Sasya

Printed in India

Contents

Introduction

That our lives, bodies and well being are related to colors, that our characters and behavioral traits can be detected by the very same colors, only strengthens the conviction that once we enter the realms of the occult we might realize the values of the most basic gifts of nature.

S.G.J Ouseley in his book "The Science of the Aura" reveals to us how one's aura reflects our soul's character, and how we are all capable of recognizing a person's true character behind what we believe to be a very plain and ordinary existence. He has told us how we are all in possession of our own personal 'auras' and how they can tell a medium of our own basic character.

Enthralling description of something we all possess but cannot view demands that we give our full attention to the subject. He even explains to those who are interested, that like the powers a yogi searches with his extreme practices of Hatha Yoga, we may also with careful practice develop the powers of discerning the auras if we so choose. This he is very careful to qualify by telling us that obviously, we may not all achieve this to the same degree. That is to say, the more adept we are the clearer they will appear to us.

It becomes very clear that whether it be Occidental or Oriental occultism and however well we may disguise it in terminology or language or even concepts which may be foreign to each other we all discuss the same thing. The variations or conceptual differences are closely related to the environments that they have evolved from. A person of Chinese origin may have a totally different view of a subject to shall we say a European living in the centre of industrial Europe. We should therefore approach this subject with very open minds and be prepared to allow the author to lead us like children along the path he lays out to achieve and learn whatever we may about this subject.

CHAPTER I

The Human Atmosphere

Of all branches of Occult Science one of the most interesting is the study of the *Aura*. Speaking concisely, the aura is a subtle, magnetic emanation generated by the etheric and other forces of the being or object with which it is connected.

Everything in nature generates its own aura, atmosphere or magnetism. The fact is equally true of the lowest crystal and of the living organism, of the lowest and of the highest conscious entity.

To illustrate this point let us consider the common magnet. Around its poles there exists a sphere of influence known as the magnetic field through which pass lines of force between one pole and the other.

The existence of this field is known by the influence of the magnet upon light iron filings when these are placed at random on a sheet

1

of paper and they will respond to the magnet which is held beneath them without contact and will follow the motions of the magnet. If these small filings are polarized by the magnet there is a remarkable affinity in their motion—they become temporarily imbued with magnetic power.

Supposing that these filings possessed intelligence and could be interrogated, they would probably say that they moved because they desired to do so—they readily followed an irresistible impulse. They would not be conscious of the real source of power. The more sensitive the filings the greater would be the distance at which their response would take place—consequently the more sensitive would respond readily to impacts which would make no effect upon the grosser filings. Movement of an electrical circuit across these lines of magnetic force converts the motion into power, and this power may be transformed into light, heat, or other forms of energy. This phenomenon is known as induction.

In the human organism there are forces analogous to, if not identical with, the forces of electricity and magnetism. Each human being possesses a "magnetic" field, which is the aura—it radiates from each individual, as solar rays emanate from the sun. The human aura partakes of the essential qualities of the etheric, the astral, the mental and the spiritual forces of the individual. In a vital sense, every human being creates his own magnetic atmosphere, which unfailingly reveals the temperament, disposition, character and the condition of health.

Is there any practical and scientific proof of the existence of the human aura? The answer is, its existence is evidenced in various ways. For example, when charged with high potential electricity, the aura itself becomes electrified, and if a neon or argon-filled lamp then be brought within the "sphere of influence" it lights up. The illumination occurs within a definite boundary which is variable around the body-there is a definite line of demarcation. It may be a matter of inches in one part and possibly a number of feet in another, while there may be rays which can be traced by the lamp projected in a straight line for a matter of five or six feet. In this way it is possible to make definite mapping out of the aura of an individual. Further evidence of this "sphere of influence" is provided by the researches of Dr. Kilner, which will be examined in the next chapter.

Thus auric emanation has been known to Occult scientists for a long time under a variety of names. It is the "magnetism" of Mesmer, the "electric fluid" of Jussieu, the "odylic flames" of Reichenbach, the "exteriorized sensibility" of de Rochas, the "vital rays" of Dr. Baraduc.

The researches of these scientific men

prove conclusively that all bodies, whether animate or inanimate, emit a subtle radiation. Special sensitiveness is, of course, requisite to detect subtle forces in nature and the aura, although undetected by the majority of people in ordinary states of consciousness, is detectable and clearly recognizable by individuals in subtle conditions of sensitiveness.

Clairvoyant sight has from the most ancient times testified to this subtle extension of the soul. The "halo" round the head of a saint is no poetical fiction, no more than the invisible aura or sphere of life radiating from a precious stone. Sometimes this aura, not restricted to the head, is depicted as surrounding the whole body with a misty glow or luminous cloud. When Moses came down from the Mount with the stone tablets we are told that the skin of his face "shone" so that the people were unable to look upon him. Here is ancient testimony to this aura lit up by the infinite power of spirit.

As each sun has its system of planets revolving around it, so each body is surrounded by smaller centers of energy evolving from the common center and, of course, partaking of the qualities of that centre. Copper, carbon and arsenic for instance send out auras of red; lead and sulphur emit blue auric colors; gold, silver and antimony, green; and iron emits all the colors

4

of the spectrum. Plants and animals emit similar colors according to their innate characteristics; in a later chapter it will be seen how the human aura also expressed itself by color-tones.

The student of occultism who has not gained the power of clairvoyance, may still sense the presence of the aura by feeling conscious of the strange power which some people with strong, forceful characters, carry around with them. They may not be spiritual or even intellectual people, but the very force of their personality seems to radiate from them.

The aura is just such a kind of subtle extension of the personality which is capable both of giving and receiving impressions, and through this medium we make conscious contact quite apart from the physical senses. We feel the instinctive attraction or repulsion, as the case may be, and we can give no reasons; nonetheless the attraction and repulsion speak of an intrinsic harmony or disharmony between the auras.

The explanation of the aura is to be found in the nature of man. The three basic principles, the etheric, the astral, and the mental, which constitute a human being go to form the aura. To these principles may be added the spiritual, but this belongs to a different order of consciousness although it also manifests through the aura.

Interpenetrating the physical body (and in reality a part of it) is the etheric counterpart, or "double," the "ectoplasm" that plays so large a role in the séance room. It is the vehicle of the life-forces which flow into man from the outer world— from the atmosphere, the sun, the planets, cosmic rays. It vitalizes and sustains the physical body death, as it is called, is the cessation of the functioning of the etheric body on the earth plane. Interpenetrating the etheric double is the astral body, the vehicle of the emotions, desires and passions-it is chiefly the brilliant, ever-changing radiations of the astral body that clairvoyants perceive in describing the aura. The astral body is in its turn interpenetrated by a more refined and subtle structure, termed the mind, or mental body, the vehicle of thought, usually visible to seers as a golden nimbus encircling the head.

These three bodies, layers, or zones overlap each other; the etheric body extends only a little beyond the aura; the astral body with its egg-shaped configuration forms the second aura, and the mental body, with its subtler and less defined structure, forms the outer aura. In addition to these three general auras there are still more subtle emanations depending on the development of the higher spiritual nature. In some individuals of a devout, unselfish mystical type the spiritual aura is very pronounced and beautiful, whilst in others of an animal-like nature there is no vestige of it. Nothing colors the aura like habitual thought-we shall see the reason for this in a later chapter.

The aura varies in many ways. In the first place there will be the question of its area and extent—this will depend on the development of the soul and mind. In primitive people these inner forces will naturally be crude and rudimentary while in intelligent, highly developed individuals the opposite will be true.

The composition or texture of the aura will also vary according to the individual—the brutal and the refined, the sensitive and the insensitive, the choleric and the placid will manifest different auras in accordance with their disposition and character.

The aura is further rendered complex and diversified by the varied play of the emotions, passions and feelings which impart a definite iridescence or color-tone to the auric radiations. The study of the color aspects of the aura is very interesting and instructive—it is fully dealt with in a later chapter.

The aura is also an unfailing guide to the health condition. In sound health the vital rays or forces stream into brilliance; in failing health the color tones are dull and dark, whilst disease is indicated by nebulous spots or patches over the part affected.

It is thus apparent that our true character is "photographed" on the aura; that which we intrinsically are as distinct from what we appear to be will stand revealed to the sensitive eye. In no other way in fact can be explained the attraction or repulsion we often experience on meeting people for the first time. It is the invisible play of the aura which persuades us before the spoken word or outward form.

The human atmosphere is the invisible influence at work in all kinds of contacts, business, social emotional and so on. It explains why some people are source of inspiration and personal power influencing all those who come within the sphere of their influence— the successful preacher, doctor, politician and others who are spoken of as having magnetic personalities. The lesser lights, the host of small, ordinary people are attracted and energized by their powerful auras, just as the small iron filings are irresistibly drawn into the magnet's field of influence; furthermore the auras of these "little people" may become polarized by the influence of a powerful personality and they may even become "lit up" with the brightness imparted to them. In the Bible records there are numerous cases of the transmission of spiritual powers and forces, and the transformation of lesser gifts and qualities into greater ones which cause marked changes in the aura.

Dr. Coates expresses the far-reaching effects of the aura in the following passage taken from his book "Human Magnetism;" "Some natures are so harmonious to all within their sphere. Their presence cheers and up-builds those in sympathy with them, while it has a counteracting influence upon others less well disposed. Angular, vicious, and unhappily-developed natures shrink out of such presences and refrain from evil or are won over by it to a higher and sweeter life. Then there are those who are not only giving off benign influences but are also absorbing into themselves the vibrations which proceed from higher and brighter souls dwelling in supernal planes. It is thus inspiration comes. It is within the radius of this magnetism that the inner and outward, the unseen and the seen, commingle and man reaches heaven-wards while still retaining his touch of earth."

CHAPTER II

The Scientific Basis of the Aura

The phenomena which has been described in the preceding chapter is not a new discovery. The idea of an emanation surrounding the human body is probably as old as human tradition. We find mention of the aura among the writings of the Ancients. The books of Hermes, the sacred books of the Egyptians allude to the emanation theory, and the Yogis and Oriental occult philosophers support the belief.

In the West the writings of Paracelsus and Van Helmont confirmed the ancient teaching. Paracelsus, who was one of the first Western scholars to propagate the theory of the Astral Body, held that round the physical body extended an invisible radiation or "fiery globe."

It was not until the eighteenth century that the modern scientific study of the aura began. The year 1734 saw the birth of Anton Mesmer who became one of the most ardent students of any period. Becoming a doctor of medicine he turned his attention to the subject of magnetism and became deeply interested in the then little understood forces and emanations which proceeded from steel palates and magnets. He was much impressed by the experiments of the Jesuit priest, Father Hehl, and the cures he affected by magnetism. Following out the Paracelsian law of "correspondences" and anticipating the modern theory of the electro-magnetic basis of life, Mesmer discovered that all the effects attributed to ferro-magnetism could be induced by the emanations flowing from the human hand. These human emanations he termed "animal magnetic fluid," or "Animal Magnetism." Mesmer established a clinic at Vienna and his methods of magnetic healing caused a furor of excitement. Unfortunately, Mesmer had a weakness for theatrical display – his magnetic seances became spectacles of wild enthusiasm and fanaticism. Eventually a scientific commission examined the phenomena and issued an adverse report; the commissioners stated that "they could find no proof of the existence of the animal magnetic fluid" but, as Dr. Buchanan says "If Mesmer did not know how to demonstrate scientifically an influence emanating from the human constitution, the commissioners should themselves have made a proper investigation; but they did not."

"Animal magnetism" fell into the background after Mesmer's death but certain scientists, unable to dismiss the magnetic emanations as mere illusions, continued experimenting privately. One of the foremost of these nineteenth-century back-room scientists was Baron Von Reichenbach, who announced in 1845 his discovery of a radiation from certain objects which he termed "odic force" or the "odylic flames." He asserted that it was generated by certain crystals, by magnets and by the human body, and claimed that it could be seen with the naked eye. Reichenbach worked on different methods to Mesmer, and sought to avoid theatricalism and sensationalism. He carefully selected persons whom he called sensitives; they sat in darkened rooms under quiet, calm conditions and were able to see flames, sparks, rays of light and white clouds emanating from a magnet. Different colors were perceived from the differing poles of the magnet and even from certain crystals and plants. In the course of further experiments it was discovered that certain of Reichenbach's sensitives could perceive similar emanations issuing from the human finger tips. The "odylic light" and the auric clouds were later photographed, and much interesting speculation as to the cause and origin of these normally invisible emanations was aroused.

It was not, however, until a few years before the First World War that further scientific light was thrown upon the "Aura." A remarkable book The Human Atmosphere *(Human atmosphere published 1920 by G.*

Routledge & Sons ltd.) was written by Dr. W. J. Kilner, Medical Electrician at St. Thomas's Hospital, London, In this book Dr. Kilner announced his discovery of a scientific method whereby the human atmosphere or "Aura" could be observed – Dr. Kilner's invention marked a new era for the Aura.

Dr. Kilner realized that if the magnetic radiations were really perceptible to specially sensitive sight they belonged to that order of phenomena known as the ultra-violet. This type of light is normally invisible to sight being of a wave length that is too short or of a vibratory rate that is too high for ordinary vision. Except in special circumstances the human eye unassisted cannot see beyond.

It occurred to Dr. Kilner that if the aura was a reality it should be possible to construct some kind of apparatus such as a screen to exclude certain light rays and to render visible the ultra-violet. Convinced of the possibility of this, he commenced research work and after several years succeeded in perfecting a screen. It consisted of a cell of optically-ground glass shaped like an excessively narrow box, containing an alcoholic solution of decyanin, a coal tar dye. The subject under observation, after removing the clothing, stands against a black background in a dimly-lighted room, there being just sufficient light to enable the body to be seen distinctly. The observer prepares his auric sight by gazing through the screen for a few moments at a fairly bright light, preferably a north sky on a sunny day, or in lieu of that, at a 100 watt electric bulb; then before the light coming through the dye-solution wears off, he concentrates intently on the subject.

Dr. Kilner and his associates found that every human being is entirely surrounded by a faint luminous but colorless mist extending about 18 ins. To 2 ft. in all directions and somewhat oval in shape. He noted also that this cloudy emanation varied in shape and clearness from day to day, and appeared fainter and obscure in illness. He further observed that the extremity of the aura seemed to merge into surrounding space and that the line of demarcation was difficult to define.

Interested in the medical aspect, Kilner began to apply his knowledge of the aura to methods of diagnosing disease, and in 1919 he formulated a system of auric diagnosis. The second edition of his book contains the record of numerous experiments; in particular the presence of certain diseases and maladies, such as epilepsy and hysteria, was detected, or rather indicated by certain peculiarities in the aura. It was also discovered that some subjects, more especially women, could produce changes in the aura by an effort of will, causing rays to issue from the body or the color of the aura to alter.

Certain pathological conditions also affected the shape and appearance of the aura—at some points the oval mist bulged, at others it lost its proper proportions, whilst sometimes dark patches appeared.

Such phenomena is quite understandable in the light of occult science which draws attention to the fact that the emanations perceived by Dr. Kilner comprised chiefly the Etheric Aura. The Etheric Body is the centre or vehicle of the vital forces in man is thus of paramount importance as regards the health. In the Etheric Body the complicated chemical, biological and magnetic principles are dynamically active. During health the Etheric radiates in straight lines in every direction, but in ill-health, when the Etheric Body becomes attenuated it is not able to draw to itself the same amount of force. Then the lines of vital magnetism appear feeble and bent, indicating the depleted condition. In health the great force of these radiations counteract germs and bacteria which are inimical to the physical health, but in sickness these auric emanations do not so easily eliminate disease germs; hence disease germs may easily enter and produce harmful effects.

Dr. Kilner also observed the curious fact that a strong positive aura reacted upon the weak, negative kind as a fully charged battery will disseminate its charge if connected to weaker ones. On the other hand a weak, depleted aura, indicating reduced vitality, acted as a psychic sponge or "vampire" on those around and sapped their energy.

It is interesting to note that there are certain cases where the Ehteric Body leaves the physical organism and withdraws the vitality, such as when a hand or leg seen by clairvoyants hanging outside the physical arm or leg until the vitality re-enters the temporary "dead" limb. Sometimes in hypnosis the head of the Etheric Body divides and hangs outside the physical head, one half over each shoulder, or lies around the neck like a collar. When anesthetics are used the Etheric Body is partially driven out and if the application is too strong and prolonged death results.

It has been found that the effect of using the decyanin screen is cumulative and that after a time it may be dispensed with. Practice in observation greatly develops the power of auric sight. Some observers, following Kilner's method, state that they see a narrow black (transparent) band between the body and the aura, of a bluish-grey misty appearance; by observing the aura through a screen containing a dilute solution of carmine they claim that it can be divided into two distinct portions, the inner portion presenting a striated appearance, the outer being obscure and nebulous.

Many people are somewhat vague as to
what exactly the decyanin is. Briefly, it is a
remarkable quinoline dye of highly complex
constitution made by an elaborate and very
costly process. The price of one tenth of a grain
(a little over three-hundredth of an ounce)
before the War was 12s. 6d. The substance
forms blue crystals which are soluble in either
water or alcohol. Solutions appear reddish
purple by transmitted light, but by reflected
light they present a very dark greenish hue.
If sufficiently diluted however, they become a
beautiful blue. The dye is used in spectro-
photographic work, as it imparts red
sensitiveness in an extraordinary degree to
silver bromide plates, for which purpose a
solution of the dye is made by dissolving *one
part of decyanin in 1,000 parts of alcohol* and
then diluting one part of this solution with 50
parts of water. These figures give some idea
of the extraordinary potency of the dye.

There is no doubt that gazing through a
decyanin screen produces an effect on the eyes.
Experiments have been carried out on a
selected object under a delicate microscope
before and after the observer has gazed
through a screen of this type; it was found that
the two readings differed, the effect of the
screen being apparently to change the focal
length of the eye rendering the observer
somewhat short sighted. Dr. Kilner's theory
of the action of the decyanin is that by

shortening our sight, it enables us to focus rays of light, such as ultra-violet rays, which are normally invisible.

It is unfortunate that Dr. Kilner's researches appear to have caused less interest in orthodox scientific circles than the importance of his demonstrations would seem to have warranted. The medical profession generally appears to have disregarded his screen. On the other hand it should be pointed out that not all occultists accept Dr. Kilner's views concerning the aura and the process whereby it becomes increasingly visible as the result of continued experiment. Some are of the opinion that Dr. Kilner was a natural clairvoyant and that his experiments with decyanin were merely the means that led to the development of his clairvoyance. To sensitives the aura will be fully manifested without any external or artificial means. On the other hand the use of the decyanin screen probably accustoms the observer to seeing the invisible and thus facilitates the development of the clairvoyant faculty, the physical emanation or aura which the decyanin makes visible being but the scryer's crystal wherein the unseen is made manifest.

CHAPTER III

Color Aspects of the Aura

We have seen that the aura is the sum-total of thought forces and emotions — etheric, astral, mental and spiritual — of the individual. We shall now see how the aura expresses itself in terms of color vibration. The basis of the study and interpretation of the aura is the fact that the thoughts and feelings collect around the physical frame in the form of fine, vibratory waves or rays of color.

Vibration is an important word. Science is discovering much about the "X" Ray, the Violet and ultra-violet ray, the Infra-red Ray and the little understood Cosmic Ray. Rays, and in fact the entire phenomena of the Universe, are the manifestations of different rates of vibration. Actually color is really vibration, possessing a symbology entirely its own. The world of nature is really a symphony of color expressing emanations of various light rays, whether it be the delicate hues of dawn, the vivid tints of sunset, the glory of the rainbow or the gleaming intensity of the midday sun in summer.

Occult Science teaches that the Central Sun emanates great vibratory rays or wave lengths of light, termed the seven major vibratory rays from which spring the seven basic main types of human mentalities and temperaments. In order of degree they comprise:

Violet – Spiritual Power.

Indigo – Intuition.

Blue – Inspiration.

Green – Energy (Supply).

Yellow – Wisdom.

Orange – Health.

Red – Life. (Secondary meanings are also attached to the auric colors)

As everyone knows these basic colors compose the Spectrum, but each of these seven great rays is divided into many sub-hues; the Violet Ray, e.g., proceeding from the shorter to longer wave-length is divided into heliotrope, amethyst, orchid, royal purple, wisteria and lavender. In addition to these science admits of many rays which are invisible to normal physical sight; as, for example, the ultra-violet.

Cosmically speaking, the aura of planets in our Solar System is based upon the same color expression as to symbolism as that of the human aura. Mars emanated red aura, Venus has a green radiation, our Earth displays a purple aura, whilst Mercury, the "Messenger of the Gods" vibrates to indigo.

The seven great vibratory rays possess an inner or occult significance which is of great importance in the study of the aura. In the human aura there are basic color-tones that reveal definite classes of talents, habits and character and there are numerous individual color-tones.

The ancient Egyptians first formulated the doctrine of the correspondence between colors and the three-fold human constitution. It was shown in the previous chapter that a human being is made up" of differing layers of consciousness or planes of being and that he possesses a separate vehicle for the expression of each of these, viz., the physical, etheric, astral, mental and spiritual bodies. Each of these bodies or modes of consciousness as they more correctly are, is related in some particular way to the three primary colors, red yellow and blue which symbolize the corporeal body (physical-etheric), the soul (astral-mental) and the spirit (spiritual consciousness) respectively. From this trinity emanates or evolves the secondary or complementary colors, viz., orange, green, indigo and violet, and by the blending of these seven major rays together with black and white all other colors are obtained.

Red

To start at the bottom of the color-scale – the Red Ray – this is predominantly the physical color. Red is the symbol of life – its presence denotes strength and vitality. People with a great deal of red in their auras have strong physical propensities, strong minds and wills, and usually a materialistic outlook on life. They often manifest a very warm and affectionate nature. Red denotes the deepest of human passions – passionate love, courage, hatred, revenge, etc.

Varying shades of Red signify different qualities. The presence of very dark, rich tones shows a tendency to selfishness. Cloudy reds are the best of the Red Group – such color tones reveal the possession of generosity and praiseworthy ambition.

Where Red suffuses the aura very heavily it shows a strong commanding nature – the type we call a "magnetic personality." It is seen in pioneers and leaders of daring enterprises.

The darker the shade of Red the less favorable are the aspects. Crimson in the aura indicates a propensity to sensuality and the lower passions and desires, whilst deep scarlet signifies lust. Deep crimson shot with black is the indication of a low, sensual nature – one whose mind is under the control of the animal passions. In all reddish auras there is an inherent tendency towards sense-

experience rather than towards the mental or
spiritual. The negative aspects of Red are seen
in the domineering and bombastic natures of
certain individuals in the group. Flattery and
vanity are further aspects of the type.

Orange

The Orange Ray comprises all shades of
orange from the dull reddish-orange denoting
selfishness and pride to the bright clear tones
of health and vitality. Orange expresses the
vital force, the energy of the sun. The Yogis
call it the "soul of energy." The presence of
strong orange hues in the aura bespeaks a
personality that is vital, energetic and active
– the "live wire" in fact. Such people frequently
dominate their fellows by the sheer force of
their vital qualities.

They are generally born for positions of
responsibility, and find it easier to rule than
to serve, but there is usually an absence of
the lust for power. They are good masters –
the type of person who tactfully manages
others. They are excellent mixers and can
usually get on with any class of person, rich
or poor. The Orange Ray is however seldom
found without a certain amount of pride which
is generally subordinated to common sense.

Ancient writers regarded Orange as
expressive of wisdom and the reasoning
powers. People coming under the Orange Ray
are usually well balanced individuals.

Yellow

Yellow, except for certain dark, muddy shades, is a good aspect in the aura. The golden shades particularly denote soul qualities, the astral-mental forces. Yellow symbolizes thought and mental concentration. Where yellow predominates it shows the presence of Intellect. It signifies light, representing the sun.

Bright, golden yellow has a spiritual significance which accounts for its use in religious ceremonies and sacred mysteries, as, for example, the use of golden vessels and altar fittings.

The Yellow Rays are most beneficial, possessing the power to dispel fear and worry. It has a tonic element which is valuable in certain forms of nervousness. It is stimulating both to health and mind.

This color appears in the auras of bright, optimistic types of people. It is seen round people who are intelligent and capable especially in business matters. The pale-yellow type are as a rule high-spirited as well as thoughtful.

The dark, dingy of yellow are bad – they denote jealousy and suspicion. Certain dull yellow hues appearing in the aura bespeak unpractical natures – people who "dream the idle hours away" in purposeless visions and useless reveries. Such people are not optimists but visionaries.

As a rule yellow shading to gold denotes a soul that is developing spiritual qualities.

Green

The presence of Green in the aura, with the exception of olive-green and certain dark shades, is a good sign. The color in general indicates Individualism, Regeneration, Energy and Supply. It is the keynote of the Ego. The Green Ray governs individual growth, as for example, the growing seed. People who have achieved prosperity and success in life invariably display strong green tints in their auras. Green also governs the mental realm and indicates a multiplicity of ideas. Bright clear green appears in the auras of people who are naturally animated, versatile, thoughtful and adaptable. It typifies freedom from bondage, independence, new life.

If nervous, highly-strung people realized the beneficial and curative effects of Green on the mind and nerves they would surround themselves with this soothing color. Its vibrations are extremely refreshing to the soul.

In the East, green is the color of mourning but this idea is based on the belief that it is the color of growth and new life rather than a symbol of death and sadness. The Chinese (a philosophical people) use Green lavishly at their festivals of joy and gladness.

The negative aspects of Green are envy and jealousy denoted by dark green and deceit and treachery by olive green.

Blue

"Heaven's own hue." Blue represents Inspiration – the spiritual color. Its spiritual power and significance have long been known. In Eastern countries blue colored objects were placed in tombs to ward off evil spirits.

In China and Japan it is the color of Fortune.

The presence of much Blue in the aura signifies an artistic and harmonious nature, and spiritual understanding. It is the Ray of the Moon and has always been associated with the feminine aspect. Blue figured prominently in the temples of Isis in Ancient Egypt. In the Roman Church it is the color of the Virgin Mary.

Bright blue denotes self-reliance and confidence it indicates a more positive character than those whose auras radiate the paler shades of blue. People with a great deal of bright blue as a rule are loyal friends, and sincere characters.

The darker shades of blue show spiritual qualities. INDIGO in the aura shows a high degree of spirituality – integrity and deep sincerity. Wisdom and saintliness are represented by dark blue auras. Certain shades of light blue indicate Idealism.

Violet

The Violet Ray is a phenomenon that is rarely seen in the average aura. It is the most highly spiritual color. Violet contains the spirituality of blue with the addition of the red elements of vitality and power. It is the color of the Initiate and the Adept – indeed it hardly belongs to the earth plane at all but to the high sphere of spiritual beings.

It has long been regarded as the Royal Color – the ray of power and influence. All great souls come under its benign dominion.

Its presence in the aura denotes true greatness and worthiness. People remarkable for their disinterested love and wisdom radiate beautiful violet color-tones. The more blue shades of purple are a sign of transcendent idealism.

Grey

People with an inborn love of convention, formality – the "red-tape mind" – have varying degrees of grey in their auras. Its presence is help to indicate a lack of imagination, a tendency to narrow-mindedness – a heavy opaque grey may be taken as showing meanness and dullness.

Some writers regard grey as denoting deep power of concentration and perseverance. Grey-aura people are certainly very persistent – the plodding type who will leave no task undone. Among these people we find the "lone wolf" and folk who love to carry out life in their own way.

Black

Beware of this "color." Strictly speaking it is not a color but the negation of color. From the most ancient times black has been associated with dark deeds and devilry, and its presence in the aura is always evil and vicious. The trend of the early churchmen and ecclesiastics to a fondness for black is not understood. The religions of the East have not made this mistake. The occult influences of black stand low in the scale; it indicates hatred, discord and evil-thoughts of all types. That most deplorable of beings whom we call a "lost soul" had a black aura denoting the loss or negation of all good.

In the most devilish and depraved souls, the aura is sometimes seen to glow with a crimson-red shot with black-the most vicious combination of evil known.

Pink

By ancient philosophers pink was regarded as a mystic color because it is neither one shade nor the other and as such could not be explained or understood. A pink aura denotes a quiet refined, modest type of character. One seldom sees pink in the aura of positive, dogmatic or aggressive people. It manifests frequently in people who like a quiet life and are fond of beauty and artistic surroundings. People of the pink-aura type will evince great and lasting devotion. The retiring and self-sacrificing nun has a strong admixture of pink with the heavenly blue of her mystic aura.

Silver

A silver-streaked aura shows the possessor to be a volatile and lively but unreliable personality. The color goes with people who are versatile, active, and gifted in all matters pertaining to movement, dabblers in all trades and professions, but masters of none! Expect feebleness, inconstancy and changeful moods where silver predominates. And be on your guard!

Brown

Brown denotes capacity for organization and orderly management. It is the business man's color. It stands for industry – for example the brown earth which ceaselessly strives to bring forth fruit and plant life. Do not expect strong emotional feelings or tendencies in brown tinged auras. It is the ruling color of convention and the "apple pie" type of mind. It is the starting point of ambition and power – material and commercial – and painstaking perseverance. When tinged with green it shows selfishness – the grabbing instinct. The lighter shades of brown indicate avarice in the possessor.

CHAPTER IV

Developing Auric Sight

A preliminary test

A simple test which the experimenter may discover whether he or she is sensitive to auric radiations may be made as follows:-

When you go to bed at night take an ordinary iron magnet with you. Having put the light out and made the room as pitch dark as possible get into bed and be relaxed for a minute or two. It is important to make your mind as passive as possible. Then holding the magnet under the bedclothes gaze steadily upon it. You must of course lift the clothes but the magnet itself should be quite invisible to you. You can tell where it is by touch. After a few moments you should be able to see a faint pale light hovering round the poses of the magnet. The light will vary in intensity according to the degree of auric clairvoyance you possess. You may see just a misty patch of light or clearly defined rays. If either phenomenon occurs it shows that you possess actual power for seeing the aura.

If you fail to see any light the first or second time don't give up. You should allow a week or a fortnight to test yourself.

This is a simple, elementary test. If you wish to develop auric sight a step further then you can experiment by concentrating your sensing faculty on another person. Choose someone with whom you are in harmony. A dark curtain or some dark unpolished material should be hung up in a quiet room on the wall opposite the window.

The subject stands or sits about twelve or eighteen inches away from the dark curtain with what little light there is falling evenly on him.

With some observers, it is preferable to have the subject as far as possible unclothed, but it is not essential.

If the experiment is being made in the daytime, you should stand at the window and gaze at the sky – not the sun – for half a minute; if after dark, it will be sufficient to gaze at the electric light for the same length of time. You should then close your eyes, sit down, relax and endeavor to become as passive as possible. Concentrate mentally on the idea of the aura. Be careful to avoid making an effort of will. Gaze calmly at the subject and note the formation of any mist, lights, or rays in any region of his or her body. Do not be easily discouraged if nothing is seen. Patient and regular practice is as necessary in developing auric sight as any other form of psychic development. Colors in the aura are not always seen objectively, but they may be "felt" or sensed.

The head seems the main field for the manifestation of the aura. It has been found that those who are above the average in mental power and alertness have a much broader and clearly defined auric base round the head than those with weak intellects. It is interesting to note that the male and female auras have different characteristics. As a rule the female aura appears larger and better developed. The rays seem capable of being influenced by the will of the person possessing them and it will be found that some women are able to project them from any part of the body, or even to change their color.

Experiment with the Hands

The subject is asked to place the finger-tips of both hands together for upwards of a minute and then slowly draw them apart. Auric radiations can be seen issuing form the tips of the fingers and uniting each hand. A small group of people can participate in this experiment. The best method is to lay an unglazed black cloth on the table. Each experimenter must relax and try mentally to visualize the aura. It will be found that some form of soft music or singing helps in bringing about the desired atmosphere. The hands rest upon the table palms downwards. When the fingers are pointed towards an experimenter opposite the etheric rays will be seen to reach across and unite.

Each pair of sitters will be seen united in the same way. Around many hands a dark line may be seen intervening between the fingers and the aura surrounding them. The outer edge of the aura emits rays of varying color and intensity. The hands of the more vital and sensitive people appear to radiate sunlight whilst others remain normal. The latter is not likely to develop but an improvement may occur by changing the sitter next to him. When auras cannot be made to blend, phenomena will not occur.

If there are several sensitives among the experimenters the aura from all hands blends in the centre like a luminous cloud composed of rapidly-moving auric particles.

Color Exercise

To develop color awareness in the seeing of auras, it is a beneficial exercise to place some strips of brightly colored paper in different envelopes. Sit in a comfortable position. Devote a few minutes to deep breathing which will bring about a state of relaxation.

Breathe deeply and slowly until no more air can be inhaled. Then hold the breath and bear the full lung pressure down on the pit of the stomach for a few seconds after which exhale gradually until the lungs are entirely emptied of air. This breathing must be done under conscious control of the mind. During the exercise visualize the seven Major Color Rays.

Make a mental picture of a globe of light which is constantly changing color. First red, then orange, yellow, green, blue, indigo and violet. After a few minutes of color concentration hold one of the envelopes in your hand or against the middle of your forehead and try to visualize the color within.

Sometimes the auric emanations will be seen to settle on the hands of one or other of the sitters – usually the most sensitive person present.

It is usual to make the first half hour of experiments in full light. In the second half hour, when concentration and practice have induced passivity, the experiments may be made in semi-darkness.

With most people auric vision does not come in a few days or even months. It is a lifetime study and one's life and habits must be on a high plane to get good results. The finer forces are not discernible to the eyes of the gross materialist or the seeker after wonders and sensations. It is not to be considered that "having eyes they see not." The study and practice of seeing the aura is not to be lightly entered upon. It is a serious and priceless power and should be utilized for the upliftment and betterment of humanity.

Appendix

The Functioning of the Aura

An extract from the lecture of Raoul de Fleuriere at the Institut Metapsychique International, Paris, May 9th, 1926.

"It is clear that, as far as my experience goes, this fluid (the aura) is the external and palpable radiation of vast and innumerable energies which constantly stream from the human being. Judging from its reactions, this fluid appears to be at the same time both material and immaterial – in it are light, heat, tremors, electric and magnetic currents, sometimes even fragrant perfumes.

The elements of this fluid are of course never equally presented: their proportions are infinitely variable according to the subjects of experiment. Generally, one or two are in the foreground, while the others remain on a secondary plane, or are sometimes even scarcely distinguishable.

The sensation of heat from the fluid is localized in the chest, heart and great arteries: its electro-magnetic reaction in the cerebellum, spinal cord, solar plexus and especially in the papillae of the hands and fingers.

As for the radiation of light which is the most powerful and wonderful of all, it affects particularly the apex of the brain, the forehead and the eyes, the last through tightly closed eyelids: for paradoxically enough I have never been able to see it by the usual means of normal sight.

In a general way, as soon as it issues from its human laboratory, I always see this fluid as having a very brilliant, exceedingly transparent, golden white appearance in intense vibration, somewhat like the quivering ground haze of summer-heat. Owing to the luminous property of the fluid, sometimes the psychical interior of a person's brain appears to me to be entirely lit up – at other times the light seems to be sifted so that you have the impression of looking at a landscape bathed in the moonlight of a fine summer night.

This fundamentally golden-white fluidic luminosity is but the synthesis of an infinity of other colors stored in its essential nature. For, just as the white solar ray, in passing through a prism is split up into seven basic colors, so this fluidic light divides up into distinct colors as soon as it enters the physico-psychical environment capable of dissociating it. As for the combinations resulting from their blending -- the colors of the rainbow in infinite mixture could not give any idea of them they are such that I frequently cannot find words to express their incredible tints and modifications. Moreover just as one has never seen two faces exactly alike so I have never met with two exactly similar fluids (auras). There are some that are gentle, agreeable, sympathetic, as delightful as the caress of a breeze in the spring, light and transparent as the azure of the sky ... On the other hand there are those which are keen, piercing, violent and repulsive: you might call them sharp as needles, lashing as a hailstorm, explosive as gunpowder, hostile as a squall, embodying as it were a soul of uneasiness and antipathy.

But of all the revealing fluids of a personality the most astonishing is perhaps the magnetic, which I so term by analogy with the action of the electro-magnet. For just as the latter attracts iron and steel, so the magnetic fluid seems to act physically on the metallic globules of the blood: and its power of attraction is so great from the moral standpoint that it seems well-nigh impossible to resist it. It is rare to meet with except in women. With them, when used by a virtuous soul, it draws all their surroundings towards the beautiful, the good and sublime: but in the case of a vicious soul, it turns its user into a woman of doom, a veritable vampire of souls and hearts, strewing her path with tragedy, misfortune and ruin.

Generally speaking, the fluid of every individual is so personal to himself that he cannot be confounded with anyone else. So much so that frequently I have been able to recognize a person five, ten or even twenty years after his visit simply by the examination of his fluidic radiation.

Once in possession of the essential elements of such or such a fluid, you are undoubtedly, documented on the person whose radiation it is. And that is understandable: for this fluid comes completely charged with the human makeup which emanates it. And so it radiates in its very essence the person's character—his passions, habits, ideas, aspirations, all that constitutes his physical, moral, intellectual and even biological existence."

Other Titles in this Series
BY PILGRIMS PUBLISHING

For Catalog & More Information, Write To:
PILGRIMS BOOK HOUSE
P.O Box: 3872, Thamel
Kathmandu, Nepal
Tel: 977-1- 424942, 425919
Fax: 977-1- 424943
Email: pilgrims@wlink.com.np
Website: www.pilgrimsbooks.com